William Charles Newbolt

St. Paul's Cathedral

William Charles Newbolt

St. Paul's Cathedral

ISBN/EAN: 9783741160011

Manufactured in Europe, USA, Canada, Australia, Japa

Cover: Foto ©Thomas Meinert / pixelio.de

Manufactured and distributed by brebook publishing software
(www.brebook.com)

William Charles Newbolt

St. Paul's Cathedral

St. Paul's Cathedral

IF there is one architectural object which more than another has succeeded in giving a character to the City of London, it is the dome of St. Paul's. We associate it with London in pictures; "within sight of the dome of St. Paul's" almost ranks with "within sound of Bow Bells," as delimiting Cockneydom. And as the visitor walks down the splendid Victoria Embankment, or threads his way eastward through the intricacies of the Strand and Fleet Street, it towers before him, now apparently on the Surrey side of the river, now straight in front of him, now bursting up

7

behind unsuspected corners. Certainly, Sir Christopher Wren accurately caught the spirit of London, the genius of its streets, and the *ethos* of its traffic when he set the cross on top of the dome, as majestic as a cupola, and as graceful as a spire.

And yet when the stranger has climbed the broad flight of steps, so curiously set askew to the grand ascent of Ludgate Hill, as he pushes open the little swing door and finds himself inside a somewhat dark and dingy building, with circular windows innocent of tracery, flat pilasters, transverse beams of stone, with the general feeling of squareness and flatness, relieved as Ruskin contemptuously says, with strings of Ribston pippins carved in stone, and innumerable cherubim, straight, as it were, from the tombstones of a graveyard—as he gazes with eyes still full of impressions derived from Westminster Abbey, and the Gothic queens of beauty which adorn our land—he is disappointed, he must own it; he almost

wishes he had continued to admire it from
the outside; his ideal is shattered.

Here at once it is necessary to ask the
visitor resolutely to close his eyes to Gothic
architecture in all its beauty, and to remember that he is studying an example of what
is called classical architecture, which, as re-
gards the exterior at all events, is considered
a masterpiece; while as to the interior,
if there is a confusion of classical and
Gothic, that is of classical forms with Gothic
feeling, we must remember that Wren was
coerced out of his own better judgment, " to
reconcile," according to his own words,
"the Gothic to a better manner of architecture." And, accordingly, if the visitor will
take his stand inside the western door, and,
gazing around him, let the majestic proportions of the building enter into his soul, he
will find a grandeur and a magnificence in
the spacious open vista, to which Gothic
architecture with all its splendid and minute
detail is sometimes a stranger.

St. Paul's Cathedral

Before we proceed to examine the many objects of interest and beauty to be found in the Cathedral, it may be desirable to take a rapid survey of the events which resulted in the existence of St. Paul's as we now see it.

Far back in the Saxon days of the seventh century, there was on this site a cathedral, which, in the end of the eleventh century, perished by the foe which has so often proved deadly to St. Paul's—fire. This was succeeded by the building known familiarly as Old St. Paul's, traces of which may be seen at the extreme east end, under the pavement of the churchyard, and on the south side amidst the grass beds of the south garden. This was longer and narrower than the present building, and was surmounted by a tall spire, the height of which—489 feet —would roughly correspond to "the Monument" set on top of the present dome. This spire was destroyed by lightning in the days of Queen Elizabeth, and was never restored;

while the whole building was much disfigured by incongruous alterations, and additions from the designs of Inigo Jones in the days of Charles I.; until the same enemy which was fatal to the first cathedral destroyed the second, and in the great fire which devastated London in 1666 St. Paul's became a complete ruin.

Only a short time elapsed before Wren was set to work to prepare designs for a new building, when restoration was found to be impossible. A phœnix carved in stone over the south transept porch is supposed to have been put there by the great architect as a memento of an incident which occurred to him as he was measuring out his new building. Having sent for a fragment of stone for the above purpose, one was brought to him on which was inscribed the word "*Resurgam*," which Wren regarded as a happy omen for his new work. It is only necessary to add further that in spite of much thwarting and opposition, he lived to execute his design, and St. Paul's has this almost unique, if not quite unique privilege, that it was built under one architect, under the direction of one master mason (Strong), in the episcopate of one Bishop (Compton), in the short space of twenty-two years.

We will now turn to look at the Cathedral in its detail, and at some of the treasures which it contains. Starting from the west end, we find on the north and south two spacious chapels. That on the south, which is entered through a fine screen, is used for the Consistory Court of the Bishop of London, and until quite recently was almost filled by the tomb of the Duke of Wellington, which we shall look at later on, in the new site, where it has been placed with great advantage to its beauty. Since its removal, the chapel has been converted into a baptistery, and contains the large classical marble font, deprived, however, of its ponderous and impracticable cover, and is used from time to time for baptisms in the families of those

connected with the Cathedral. Here is also
a fine window by Mr. Kempe, in memory of
Archdeacon Hessey.

Passing over to the corresponding chapel
on the north side, we enter through another
very handsome wooden screen into what is
generally known by the somewhat meaning-
less appellation of the Morning Chapel. This
chapel is in constant use for the daily and
early Sunday celebrations, for midday and
night services, for lectures and devotional
meetings, in fact for any religious purpose
for which the great area of the dome or the
large space of the choir would be unsuitable.
We may notice an adaptation of one of
Raphael's frescoes in mosaic over the altar,
by Messrs. Powell, and another mosaic at
the west end, in memory of Archdeacon
Hale. The solitary window in the chapel
is filled with glass in memory of Dean
Mansel, where we may detect in the inscription the somewhat unusual, but to those
who knew Dean Mansel, most appropriate

in gods and goddesses, naked heroes, winged Victories, and other Pagan symbols. These tell their own tale in pompous epitaph, and we need not weary the reader in describing them.

Out of the general number we would select a few, which may well claim our momentary attention. First of all, the monument to the memory of the Duke of Wellington, by Stevens, although still waiting for its completion, is well worthy of a careful inspection. Taken out of the chapel where it was impossible to see its full merits, it now, under the arch of the second bay of the nave at the north side, adds greatly to the general beauty of the Cathedral. We notice the vigorous allegorical figures at the side, Bravery trampling down Cowardice, and Truth plucking the tongue from Falsehold ; and the dignified pose of the recumbent hero beneath his canopy of state. One unfortunate result of moving the tomb has been to divorce it from the mural decorations in marble, which really form part of the design of the monument, and still remain on the walls of the south-west chapel, where it used to stand. While we are looking at Wellington's tomb, by simply turning round, we find ourselves face to face with Boehm's fine cenotaph to the memory of General Gordon. There are few tombs so honoured in the Cathedral as this; seldom a day passes in which no flowers or tokens of respect are laid on the resting soldier, oftentimes they are clearly the offerings of quite poor people. This is the tomb that Li-Hung-Chang visited with every token of affection in August 1896, and decorated with magnificent wreaths.

As we go on we may pause a moment to read the inscription on brass commemorating the loss of H.M.S. *Captain*, which foundered at sea in 1870, with the inventor of turret ships, Captain Cooper Coles, aboard. The inscription, besides recounting this terrible calamity, emphasises the importance of little things, when it points out that the cause of the disaster is to be attributed to an error of two feet in her design. Noticing as we pass Marochetti's angels guarding the somewhat fantastic tomb of Lord Melbourne, we stop at the vestibule as it were of the dome, by the entrance to the Lord Mayor's vestry, to read the names of the Deans of St. Paul's who have held that office since the Norman Conquest, inscribed on slabs of alabaster. There are some notable names among them, for instance, Colet, Sancroft, Joseph Butler, and not least, the present Dean Gregory, to whom St. Paul's owes so very much of her revived life and efficiency as the Cathedral of the metropolis.

At this point it will be convenient to cross over the nave to the corresponding aisle on the south side, which will enable us to complete our survey of the western division of the building. There is nothing to look at, rather the reverse, in the monuments to the west of us ; they are executed in the worst

taste, and are more ludicrous than edifying ;
we will therefore confine our attention to
the four alabaster slabs which in a corresponding position to that devoted to the
Deans, carry the names of the Bishops of
London from Restitutus, bishop in the year
314 A.D., down to Mandell Creighton, bishop
in 1897. The list is a very remarkable one,
not only in the names of distinguished men
which it contains, but also for its suggestive-
ness and historical value. This is no church
of yesterday or foundation of three hundred
years' growth, which can boast of a bishop
at the Council of Arles in the fourth century.
Mellitus in 604 carries our minds back to
St. Augustine, to St. Gregory and the Angles
in the slave market. St. Erkenwald recalls
to us the wealthy shrine of this once popular
saint. St. Dunstan recalls the vigorous
ecclesiastic of the tenth century. The
troublous times of the Reformation are
visible in the double record of Bonner, with
Ridley's name interposed, in the years 1540–

1553. Here is the honoured name of William
Laud, and also of Juxon, who stood on the
scaffold with Charles I. Here is Compton,
whose name is inseparably associated with
the present building, and a quartette of
bishops famous and familiar to this genera-
tion, Blomfield, Tait, Jackson, and Temple.
It is surprising to see how much interest is
manifested in this simple list by people who
pause to read it, as they pass backwards and
forwards, or take the favourite climb to the
upper galleries through the door on the
right.

Going on eastward we stand and look
up into the dome. This is not the actual
lining of the external dome, as many are
disposed to think at first sight. "It is
a shell of a different form from the outer
structure, with a brick cone between it and
the outer skin." In one sense there are
three coverings, in varying heights, one
above another ; above which again are the
lantern, the upper cupola, the gilt cross and

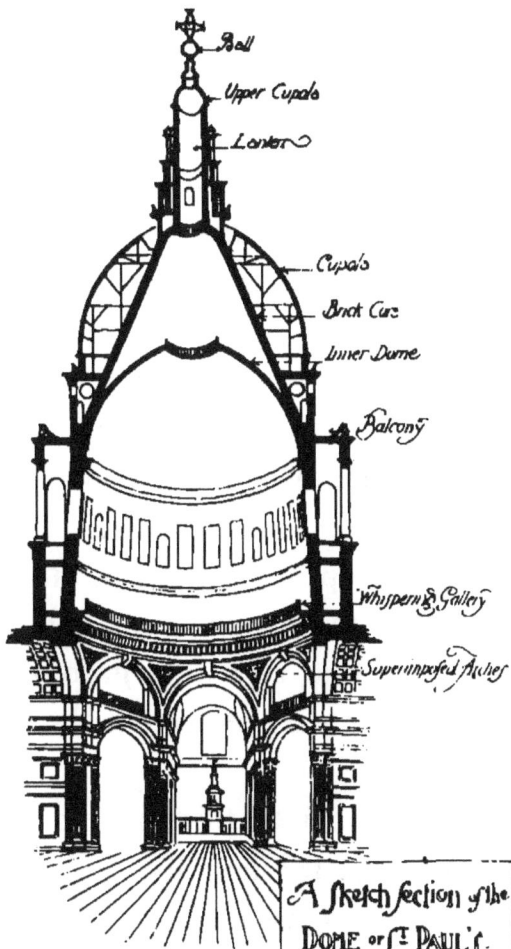

Ball

Upper Cupola

Lantern

Cupola

Brick Cone

Inner Dome

Balcony

Whispering Gallery

Superimposed Arches

A Sketch section of the DOME of St PAUL'S.

St. Paul's Cathedral

ball. As we look round this splendid feature
of Wren's great building, we cannot fail to
be struck with a similarity of feeling and
arrangement between this wide open space
with its soaring roof, and that which is the
glory of Gothic Ely, its magnificent lantern.
Indeed, there is a tradition that Wren drew
in the inspiration of this part of his work
from his acquaintance with the lovely cathedral of the fens, of which his uncle, Matthew
Wren, was bishop, and which he himself, if
truth must be told, sadly disfigured by his
attempts at Gothic, and incongruous classic
insertions, which may be seen at the present
day.

As we look up into this inner dome, we
catch a glimpse through the misty gloom,
which seldom seems to be absent, of the
paintings executed by Sir James Thornhill,
contrary to Wren's wishes, in monochrome.
They are dark and dingy, but not without
vigour and boldness of design, and represent
scenes from the life of St. Paul, broken up

by heavy architectural ornaments. At one time there was a scheme for superseding these with more modern paintings, which, happily, was never carried out. Those who penetrate the inner recesses of the Cathedral will come across designs of Lord Leighton and others now idly decorating a blank wall, which were originally submitted for the purpose. Apart from the objection there would be to destroying history, it must be felt that any attempt at decoration at this great height, and under the atmospheric conditions which prevail, would be money thrown away, and possibly a loss of mystery and elevation in the feeling of the dome as an architectural feature. As we bring our eyes down from the dusky surface of Thornhill's pictures, we notice between the thirty-two Corinthian pilasters which surround the inner space, in the intervals not pierced by windows, eight large images, which have been lately put in position, representing the four Western and the four Eastern doctors of the Church—St. Ambrose, St. Augustine, St. Jerome, St. Gregory; and St. Chrysostom, St. Gregory, St. Basil, St. Athanasius. These are strongly held in position, as they, not only in appearance, but in reality, slightly bend over the area beneath. Underneath them is the drum, at present bare, but shortly, it is to be hoped, to be bright with mosaic, offering as it does quite the most prominent field for decoration in the church. Below this again is the far-famed whispering gallery, which is said to owe its magical properties to the accident of its construction, not to design. Below this once more are the first attempts at colour decoration in the spandrels, executed by Salviati from designs by Mr. G. F. Watts R.A., and others. They represent the four evangelists and the four greater prophets, treated in a flowing, somewhat boisterous, style, which fits in, not inharmoniously, with the general architecture.

Wren has been severely criticised for "the

four superimposed arches which, alternating
with the great arches that open into the four
limbs, help them to support the dome." It
remains to be seen whether it is possible to
turn these into decorative features under the
magic skill of Mr. Richmond. Already he
is engaged in placing in mosaic, on the four
concave ceilings underneath the quarter
domes, four scenes from what may be called
the Pauline gospel of 1 Cor. xv. 3, &c.—
"For I delivered unto you first of all
that which I also received, how that Christ
died for our sins according to the Scriptures.
And that He was buried, and that He rose
again according to the Scriptures. . . . And
last of all He was seen of me also, as of one
born out of due time." So that the dome
will be reared up, as it were, on the Gospel
according to St. Paul.

Before we finish our inspection of this
part of the Cathedral, we may recall the
well-known story of the value of presence of
mind. It is said that while Thornhill was

engaged in the painting of the cupola, as ·
described above, he stepped back with an
artist's pride to examine his paintings, and
in another moment would have fallen over
the edge of the scaffolding, when a workman
with great promptitude threw a brush full of
paint at the picture, and in rushing forward
to save his work Thornhill also saved his
life.

The dome never looks so magnificent as
when it is filled with the huge congregations
which assemble here at the services on
Sundays and other days. Few clergy can
look unmoved from the marble pulpit at the
sea of heads which reaches right away into
the nave and transepts, and brings out the
vast scale of the building, which its exquisite
proportions tend to conceal.

Passing through the south transept aisle,
we notice in front of us, a window by Mr.
Kempe put in to commemorate the recovery
of the Prince of Wales and his thanksgiving
at St. Paul's in 1872, the subject chosen

Choir stalls and Organ.

being "the Raising of the Widow's Son."
Here in corners and nooks we come across
single statues of heroes and distinguished
men, and groups of allegorical figures, the
most conspicuous being Nelson and Corn-
wallis. Here we find John Howard with his
prison key, flanked on the opposite side of
the dome by a half-clothed figure of Dr.
Johnson, which legend reports to have been
mistaken for images of St. Peter and St.
Paul. Leaving this unworthy collection of
monuments, albeit to the memory of some
of our greatest men, we pass through one of
the beautiful screens of ironwork, in which
the Cathedral is so rich, and enter the south
choir aisle, close by the door of the Dean's
Vestry. There are several objects of interest
to detain us, as we pass along the back of
the magnificent stall-work, which supports a
gallery on the top. This gallery is sometimes utilised for orchestral services, or is
filled with the overflow of the congregation
on great occasions, musical and otherwise.

St. Paul's Cathedral

The stalls and their appendages, however, will be better examined presently from the floor of the choir ; let us now look at the different objects ranged along the south wall. Here is a small collection of relics from Jerusalem, including a fragment from Herod's Temple, and a piece of carved stone from the Holy City, tesselated pavement from the same city, and a small piece of stone from Mount Calvary. The monuments of ecclesiastics are also for the most part of a much more worthy character than those in the nave. Here we see the marked personality of Dean Milman ; the elder Mr. Richmond's portraiture of Bishop Blomfield. Here Woolner has produced a painful, death-like representation of Bishop Jackson, and Heber's kneeling figure executed by Chantrey is now turned towards the sanctuary. But perhaps in some ways the most interesting tomb in all the Cathedral is the strange weird figure set in the wall, whose position, however, renders inaccurate the concluding

Iron Grille
to Choir Aisle

line of the Latin inscription : " Here, though set in dust, he beholdeth Him whose name is the Rising." It is Donne, the poet dean, who presided over the Cathedral from 1621 to 1631. Hare, in his " Walks about London," describes the incident of the dean sitting for his portrait dressed in his shroud, which he preserved afterwards as a grim *" memento mori,"* and which was eventually worked into the design of his tomb. He now appears before us in his grave-clothes curiously gathered up into a sort of crown, rising from an urn, which poetically contains his ashes. Not the least interesting point in this tomb is to notice on the white marble the evident marks of fire, which show it to have stood the ordeal of the great catastrophe of 1666. This is the only tomb out of Old St. Paul's which is anything like intact. There are some few headless or legless remains gathered in the crypt, and set as decently as possible on stone bases. Yet of the bishops and distinguished men once commemorated here, all memorial has perished; Erkenwald with his famous shrine, Duke Humphrey, Deans Colet and Nowell, Vandyke, Sir Philip Sidney, and many more, are, as far as their tombs are concerned, as if they had never been. However much the fire may have to answer for, we fear the want of piety towards the past must have even more laid to its account. Certainly a clean sweep of history such as that which has taken place in St. Paul's, whatever be the cause, is much to be deplored.

We stand now, before we enter the choir, to examine thoroughly the magnificent gates which shut in on either side the north and south bays of the sanctuary. These are partly old and partly new—that is to say, the original gates by Tijou, which once stood across the choir surmounted by the organ, have been readapted, reproduced, and reset in gilded frames, from the design of Messrs. Bodley & Garner, executed by Messrs. Barkentin & Krall. The exquisite lace-like work is well worthy of a careful examination, while a curious fact may be told about their modern adaptation. It became, as we have indicated, necessary to enlarge the gates for their present position, and to reproduce a whole valve on each side. At first this presented great difficulty, by reason of the constant splitting of the foliated parts. A reference to old records, however, showed that the original gates were made of charcoal-smelted iron (the last iron used out of the Sussex Weald), and iron smelted in this way was accordingly procured from Norway, and the difficulty vanished. This may fairly rank with the two-feet error in the ship *Captain* described above, as illustrating the importance of little things, when we see a great artistic difficulty surmounted by a piece of charcoal.

Passing through the gate on the southern side, we find ourselves in the choir immediately in front of the altar. Here we cannot fail to be struck with the exceeding beauty and magnificence all around us. The choir of St. Paul's only needs one thing to make it perhaps the most beautiful work of its kind in the world ; and that, alas ! neither money nor skill can command. Were there only sunlight, such sunlight as we do get at rare intervals in the murky atmosphere of London, the blaze of colour and the exceeding wealth of design would be quite dazzling. As it is, we must follow its beauties as best we may, and if we are favoured with a bright day be thankful ; if not, at least try to appreciate the artistic excellences which are so lavishly displayed around us.

It will be convenient first to study carefully the reredos, which was erected in 1888 from the designs of Messrs. Bodley and Garner. A good deal of opposition was aroused at the time against this magnificent design, chiefly on doctrinal grounds, largely arising from unjust suspicions and supposed idolatrous emblems which in reality found no place in the work. When we remember that the east window, which the reredos superseded, and which is now in the south transept, represented in even a more realistic way the same subject of the Crucifixion, we can see how unreasonable the opposition really was; while the objection to another figure on the reredos arose from descriptions of the group which had no foundation in fact, and were only the product of a heated imagination. Whatever we may think of the reredos doctrinally and artistically, there is no doubt that it is full of teaching in a building where some of the poorest and most ignorant habitually assemble for warmth and shelter; who need something striking and appealing, to remind them of a Saviour who died to save them, and who loves them still in all their waywardness and sorrow.

The text of the sermon which the reredos is meant to teach is carved in gilt bronze letters across a frieze of rosso-antico—*Sic Deus dilexit mundum*—"So God loved the

The Choir
St Paul's

world." Here is set forth the great love
of God in the Incarnation and the Atone-
ment.

Accordingly a glance right and left at the
two extreme columns of the colonnade which
leads up to the centre piece, will show us on
the north the angel Gabriel, on the south the
Blessed Virgin; the two together forming
the opening mystery, as it were, of the
Annunciation. Looking upwards to the top
of the central structure, we see a figure of
our risen Lord, who has triumphed over
death; underneath is the Holy Child in His
mother's arms; on the right and left are St.
Paul and St. Peter, who, generally associated
together as they are, in dedications and otherwise, would, it is thought, with greater pro-
priety have been separated in this particular
case—as St. Paul is represented in London
by his own cathedral, and St. Peter by his
abbey at Westminster. There is a traditional
use about these things which in this particular
has been departed from. Coming to the

central panel, we see a representation of the Crucifixion, with a group of figures round the cross, while beneath, there are three panel subjects in low relief, representing the Nativity, the Entombment, and the Resurrection, separated by figures of angels bearing the instruments of the Passion. Beneath again there is a solid basement, pierced north and south with doors, closed with gates of light brass. The one surmounted with "*Vas Electionis*"—"The chosen vessel" of St. Paul: the other with "*Pasce oves meos*"—"Feed my sheep" of St. Peter. The whole structure is about seventy feet high, of white Parian marble, with an addition of colour gained by the use of various slabs and bands of different hues, rosso-antico, verde di Prato and Brescia marble, with a somewhat free use of gilding. The marble steps and pavement of the sanctuary form part of the same design, and are of great beauty and costliness.

The altar itself is of ebony and brass,

recalling somewhat the treatment in Torre-
giano's masterpiece in Henry VII.'s chapel
at Westminster. The altar cross is also ex-
tremely magnificent, inlaid with *lapis lazuli*
and precious stones, and the silver-gilt
candlesticks are of beautiful design. If our
visit takes place at any of the great festivals
we must not fail to notice the elaborate
needlework of the altar frontal, worked by
the East Grinstead sisters, representing scenes
in the life of St. Paul.

On the plane of the sanctuary stand two
splendid reproductions of the copper candlesticks which a constant tradition says used
to stand in old St. Paul's. The originals,
four in number, may be seen in the
cathedral church of St. Bavon in Ghent,
to which they were sold in the days of
the Commonwealth, for what they would
fetch, to replenish the Exchequer. We
should notice their elaborate workmanship,
and the royal arms of England upon them,
which goes to support an ingenious theory

South Front
St. Pauls

which now seems fairly verified, that the
original four candlesticks were included in a
design which was made for his tomb by
order of Henry VIII., by the Florentine
Benedetto da Rovezzano, of which more
will be said presently, when we get into the
crypt.

Here also are about to be placed two
magnificent candelabra, if that is the right
term, which will be used for gas or electric
light, representing all the works of Creation,
over which the light will burst out as
from a rose of glory, to illuminate the
sanctuary.

We shall now do well to examine the
famous stall-work of Grinling Gibbons, perhaps the finest of its kind in the world ;
noticing the curious closets or pews behind ;
the two Bishops' seats, the Lord Mayor's
seat, as one of the trustees of the Cathedral,
the splendid organ-case, and the by no
means inferior modern work lately placed in
the sanctuary.

St. Paul's Cathedral

But now it is time carefully to study the new mosaic work which, under the inspiring genius of Mr. Richmond, has at length wrought out the desire of Wren's heart, that St. Paul's should glow with colour, and that in imperishable mosaic. There is not space at our disposal to enter as fully as might be desired into the really great work which has been going on without interruption since 1891. Mr. W. B. Richmond started on the work with an enthusiasm for St. Paul's dating from childhood, a knowledge of Italian methods dating from his youth, and a special knowledge of the earlier methods studied at Ravenna. He has accordingly departed from the modern method, with which in England we have been lately familiarised— of a smooth surface, in which pictures are produced in mosaic as if they were painted on canvas—and has gone back to the rough, broad method, in which every cube is placed separately in the wall, care being taken so to arrange them that they shall catch the light, and be set in the manner which will most give depth and brilliancy. This method has been completely successful, and has resulted in an effect both splendid and artistic; while we have the satisfaction of knowing that every inch of the work has been done in London by English workmen, from the firm of Messrs. Powell at White-friars.

It is not a little difficult to describe so vast and so minute a work. The visitor will do well to take his stand at the entrance gate of the choir, where it is entered from the nave, and look straight forward at the roof of the apse behind the reredos. There he will see a large figure of our blessed Lord in majesty, "*Rex tremendæ majestatis*," seated on the rainbow throne, supported on the wings of the wind, to judge all nations. On His right hand angels are steadfastly gazing into an unfolded scroll, in which are recorded the names of the blessed, whom others are welcoming to glory. On His left (the spectator's right) angels are looking into the same scroll in vain for the names of the lost, and others are waiting behind to punish and expel.

Coming forward from this the eye passes along the magnificent sweep of the roof, with its three shallow saucer-domes, supported by angels in the pendentives, with appropriate inscriptions above and around them. In these three domes are three acts of Creation : the creation of birds in the easternmost, the creation of the fish and sea monsters in the centre, and the creation of the beasts in the westernmost, nearest to the great dome. These will repay a very careful inspection ; they are full of detail and splendid colour, and with the gold and red enrichment of the ribs and flat surfaces, give an effect of gorgeous and magnificent brilliancy. On each side, north and south, we see three bays all treated in a uniform manner, and all carrying out a continuous design. There is the arch, delicately picked out in colour ;

there are the spandrels over the arch ; there
is the great cornice, brilliant in red and gold,
enriching the white Portland stone. Above
these are the panels of the triforium stage,
ornamented with mosaic, and above them
again a clerestory with flat panels on either
side of the window, filled with large mosaic
pictures.

Beginning with the spandrels on the
north-west, we have the Creation of
Light and the Annunciation, balanced on
the south by the Expulsion and the Fall.
The spandrels north and south in the sanctuary are filled with warrior angels holding
the emblems of the Passion.   In the triforium
panels, above the cornice, each bay is deter-
mined by the subject of the dome which
surmounts it : Adam and Eve occupy the
north and south, with animals around them ;
fish and sea monsters are in the centre ; and
peacocks under the cupola which carries the
birds, while the different designs are separated
by flowing arabesques, or, as in the apse, pro-

longed into symbolical figure subjects, which complete the scheme. In the large panels again on each side of the clerestory, taking those on the north, we have the indirect preparation for Christ's coming, Job and Abraham, Cyrus and Alexander, the Delphic and the Persian Sibyls ; while on the south we have the different temple builders : Jacob beholding his vision of the house of God ; Moses on Mount Sinai, seeing the pattern of the Tabernacle ; Bezaleel and Aholiab ; with Solomon and David to finish the line. The composition is bound together by texts which would need a long and careful study ; while as a piece of artistic work it stands almost unrivalled in church decoration. We should notice also the curiously designed windows, which are an attempt to solve the problem, with no slight degree of success, how to produce a beautiful scheme of colour, and yet not obscure the light of day, which is so scantily admitted in London under the most favourable circumstances.

St. Paul's Cathedral

Passing out through the north-eastern screen, we find ourselves in the choir aisle leading to the chapel behind the great reredos. This has lately been fitted up and decorated, and is now known as the Jesus Chapel. The three splendid windows by Mr. Kempe are all treated with this idea. The reredos, which consists of an adaptation of a picture by Cima in the National Gallery, is set in a marble framework, and is part of a memorial to Dr. Liddon, whose recumbent effigy rests on an artistic monument under the south wall of the apse. The inscription which runs round the plinth is of great beauty; it is as follows: "Mementote fratres fratris in Christo Henrici Parry Liddon, ecclesiæ hujusce cathedralis canonici et cancellarii, animam ejus commendantes Domino quem fide constantissima Redemptorem atque Regem, Deum verum de Deo vero adoravit, dilexit, prædicavit, expectat nunc de cœlo rediturum. Decessit die ix Septembris,

St. Paul's Cathedral

anno Domini MDCCCXCmo, ætatis suæ
lxii."

It is time now to pass to the crypt and to
the upper galleries of the Cathedral. The
crypt is entered out of the south transept
aisle, and the visitor finds himself after
descending a flight of steps in a spacious
vaulted under-church, which in old St. Paul's
was known as the Church of St. Faith. One
solitary portion of this old church of the
crypt still remains beneath the level of the
churchyard at the south east of the Cathedral.
It was here that during the Great Fire books
and papers and valuables were stored out of
reach, as it was fondly hoped, of the devour-
ing flames—a hope, however, destined not to
be realised, for the blaze consumed every-
thing, and the ashes are said to have been
wafted as far as Eton. At the extreme east
end, the Confraternity of Jesus used to meet
in the Jesus chapel, and outside was the
tower containing the Jesus bells, which are
said to have been staked at dice and lost by

Nelson's Tomb in Crypt

St. Paul's Cathedral

Henry VIII. to Sir Giles Partridge. There are several tombs which may detain us for a moment as we pass along. We see on our left the memorial slab to Sir John Goss, with the first bars of the anthem which he composed for the Duke of Wellington's funeral inscribed upon it. The Transvaal and its ill-fated heroes are commemorated on a very poor brass. And Rennie, who built Waterloo and Southwark Bridges; Landseer; the special newspaper correspondents who fell in the Soudan campaign; Palmer, Charrington and Gill, who were murdered in the Sinai Desert, all claim a passing notice, as we move on to the Painters' Corner.

Here we notice the simple tomb of the great genius to whom the present St. Paul's owes its erection. Sir Christopher Wren reposes under a plain slab bearing his name and age and his claims to honour. The advanced age to which he attained, in those troublous times and out of a much thwarted life, shows a greatness of mind which could

endure all and surmount all for ninety-one
years. Above him is the original of the
famous inscription, which also reappears in
the north transept : "*Lector, si monumentum
requiris circumspice.*" Round him, or rather
at his feet, head, and side, lie many distinguished men. Leighton and Millais are
close beside him ; then comes Turner, the
prince of landscape painters, with his quaint
personality and strange whims, now desiring
that he should be wrapped in his "Carthage"
as in a shroud, now desiring that his pictures
should openly challenge comparison with
those of Claude, and hoping that he might
be buried near the great Sir Joshua Reynolds,
from whom he is separated only by another
grave. His, too, is an honoured name, the
great portrait-painter, on whose canvas live
the beauty and the grandeur and all that was
most distinguished in his day. Here, too,
are Opie and West and Lawrence and Landseer's graves. Here, more lately interred, Sir
Edgar Boehm, famous for the Jubilee coinage.

St. Paul's Cathedral

We must not linger, however, but pass on into the crypt chapel, where the simple altar rests under the apse on an effective mosaic pavement. The modern sepia windows deserve notice, and Dean Milman's grave is also a prominent object. On the north is the aisle once assigned as a burying-place to the parishioners of St. Faith, now used partially as a vestry for the gentlemen of the choir. This contains the first tomb placed in the new St. Paul's ; and here, too, may be seen the gigantic cover of the font, which only a short time ago was closely cemented down, effectively precluding all baptisms. Here we notice also, with its ever fresh tribute of flowers, Dr. Liddon's grave, immediately under the high altar.

And now going westward, we find ourselves, after passing through an iron gate, in the Wellington chapel, where the body of the hero reposes inside a huge sarcophagus made of two blocks of Cornish porphyry. There is a simple grandeur about the tomb

Wellington
Monument

which accords well with the character of the
Iron Duke. The floor is inlaid throughout
with Roman mosaic said to have been made
by the convicts at Woking. Still going
westward we reach Nelson's tomb in the
very centre of the building, where, looking
up through a grating, the eye can just catch
a glimpse of the high windows in the lantern
of the cupola. In some ways it suggests a
comparison with Napoleon's tomb at the
Invalides. The history attaching to this
marble monument is most curious, and has
been worked out with great ingenuity and
research by a Fellow of the Society of
Antiquaries. The black marble sarcophagus
long attributed, but erroneously, to Torre-
giano, formed part of an elaborate composition designed by Benedetto at the command
of Cardinal Wolsey for the purposes of his
own tomb; most probably his own effigy
once lay on the top of the black marble.
On Wolsey falling into disgrace, the whole
tomb, with its marble and bronze, was seized

by Henry VIII., and, the design considerably
amplified, was set up in what is now the
memorial chapel at Windsor (then Wolsey's
chapel), with probably the candlesticks, which
we have described above, as part of the
screen around it, and with a brazen effigy of
the king recumbent on the marble. This
was never finished, in spite of sundry efforts
and good wishes on the part of the king's
children. And under the Commonwealth it
was broken up, and all the brass or bronze
was sold for what it was worth. The
marble portion of the tomb appears to have
remained in the chapel at Windsor until the
days of George III., and then, either out of a
sense of honour to be conferred or economy
to be practised, to have been used for the
monument to Lord Nelson, whose viscount's
coronet now occupies the place once filled
by the effigy of a cardinal, perhaps also that
of a king. He himself lies underneath,
buried, as tradition says, in a coffin made
out of a mast of the French ship *L'Orient*,

which was burned and sunk by one of Nelson's captains, who presented to him the mast as the material for his future coffin.

There is not much to detain us further as we pass westward to look at the Duke of Wellington's funeral car. On either side are the workshops of the Cathedral, and its simple but most effectual warming apparatus. The ponderous carriage which stands at the west end is now shorn of its glory considerably. It has lost its velvet pall and decorations, but if somewhat barbaric, is yet a rather fine conception. It is made out of gun-metal ; a cannon out of every victory the Duke won is said to be melted down into it. Round it may be seen the plaster-of-Paris candelabra which were used for the lying in state at Chelsea. As we turn to go back down the crypt, do not let us fail to note its beautiful proportions, and the splendid way in which, in spite of the numerous visitors, it is kept.

Remounting to the floor of the Cathedral

there is still much for the visitor to see
upstairs, and much which he will never see
without a special order and guide, in intricate
passages and rooms, which are quite hidden
away from the view of the ordinary sight-
seer. Here, after ascending a tedious flight
of shallow steps, we come to the library,
where Bishop Compton's portrait looks down
on the collection which his liberality was
instrumental at least in commencing. Here,
too, is the tower containing great Paul, with
its weight of sixteen tons, and the Phelps
bell, which is only rung for the death of
certain great personages. If he is fortunate
the visitor may now see the geometrical
staircase, the clock, and the twelve bells
(with a special order), the model of St.
Paul's, and the trophy-room. Returning
again he mounts more stairs to the Whispering Gallery. If it is fine he may go still
higher and get a view of London from the
"stone gallery," or higher still from the
"golden gallery," and the ball.

St. Paul's Cathedral

Here we must leave our friends to descend the 365 steps to the floor, and to take as they depart a last look at the mighty pile, which in its vigorous religious life is no longer merely a show-place for enterprising tourists, but in the true sense of the word a place of worship.

.

Printed by BALLANTYNE, HANSON & Co.
London & Edinburgh

www.ingramcontent.com/pod-product-compliance
Lightning Source LLC
Chambersburg PA
CBHW021544270326
41930CB00008B/1357